Made in United States
North Haven, CT
02 May 2023

36176818R00057